Original title:
Stars, Bars, and Mars

Copyright © 2025 Creative Arts Management OÜ
All rights reserved.

Author: Elliot Harrison
ISBN HARDBACK: 978-1-80567-761-1
ISBN PAPERBACK: 978-1-80567-882-3

Celestial Chronicles

Up in the sky, a light so bright,
A lizard in the night, what a sight!
He leaps from one cloud to another,
Screaming, 'I'm space's favorite brother!'

A comet flew by with a squeaky sound,
Joking with planets all around.
They giggled and twirled in cosmic dance,
While clumsy craters lost their chance.

A rocket ship zoomed, full of cheese,
As aliens gathered with utmost ease.
They threw a party with snacks and drinks,
Wobbling on twilight as everyone blinks.

Balloons made of gas, so light and free,
Wondrous fun in this galactic spree!
With laughter echoing through the void,
This is how boredom's truly destroyed!

Mysteries of the Cosmos

In the sky, bright dots dance in line,
Making wishes on a dime.
Maybe they're lost, just like my keys,
Floating 'round with foolish ease.

Planets wobble, take a spin,
Wonder if they'll ever win.
Gravity pulling, making a fuss,
Hope no one spills their cosmic bus.

Constellations and Conflicts

Little shapes connect the dots,
A dog, a cat, or even pots!
Arguing over who is right,
Just a twinkling cosmic fight.

Orion's belt's gone out for tea,
While Gemini snickers by a tree.
They laugh and roll, 'til they fall,
In a never-ending cosmic brawl.

Midnight Murmurs

Whispers float on a midnight breeze,
A comet sneezes, 'Oh, excuse me, please!'
The Milky Way spills a joke or two,
While aliens chuckle, forming a crew.

Saturn's rings spin like old vinyl,
Dancing to beats that are quite primal.
Whenever they're bored, they start to spin,
Sending the cosmos in fits of grin.

Orbiting Thoughts

Circling round with silly cheer,
A thought escapes, I hold it dear.
Pluto pouts, 'I'm still a star!'
While Jupiter's gas gives off a fart.

Eclipses make a dramatic show,
But who really needs that kind of glow?
The universe giggles in grand delight,
In this curious dance of cosmic light.

Scars of the Universe

In a galaxy, not too far,
A cow once jumped over a car.
It landed with a cosmic thud,
Leaving behind a field of mud.

Aliens giggled with delight,
Drawing maps in the dead of night.
They plotted a route for a cow parade,
While bets on milk started to cascade.

Ambiguous Horizons

A rogue comet wore a tutu,
Trying to dance, but fell like goo.
With twinkling lights and overzealous flair,
It bounced off planets with no care.

The moon looked on, a little confused,
"Is this a party?" it mused and snoozed.
While over in the Milky Way's bar,
Martians mixed drinks and sang bizarre.

Celestial Shadows

Meteor showers spilled like confetti,
As rogue robots turned all quite petty.
They dropped balloons in swirling space,
Poking fun at gravity's embrace.

Jupiter's storms heard the ruckus,
While Venus rolled her eyes, quite circus.
And Saturn's rings flung jokes around,
Laughing so hard, they drooped to the ground.

Cosmic Echoes

In the great void, echoes roam,
Seeking a voice, they call it home.
"Hey Pluto, you're a planet!" they croon,
But he just replies, "I prefer a tune."

With each bounce, a chuckle rings,
As comets wear outlandish things.
Gravity's jokes take time to unfold,
Making us laugh till we're old and bold.

Wanderer's Dreams

In the night, a laugh I find,
With space snacks and cosmic wine.
I drift on beams of silly light,
Chasing comets, oh what a sight!

Galaxies dance, they beckon me,
In my ship made of jubilee.
Floating on giggles, I plot my course,
With every quirk, I feel the force!

Metaphysical Roads

On roads that twist and turn, I roam,
With jellyfish in a pickle dome.
The trees wear hats of cosmic cheese,
I wave to ants on roller skates, if you please!

Quantum puns in every bump,
A cosmic joke makes me jump.
Destination? Who can say!
I'm just here for the interstellar play!

Chasing Infinity

A foot race with time, can you believe?
My shoes are made from lunar weave.
I trip on the echoes of the past,
With dreams so big, they just won't last!

Slips and trips on space-time turf,
Laughter bursts with every surf.
I run with the moon, oh what a feat,
A cosmic chase with a candy treat!

Celestial Serenades

Sing to the void, oh what a tune!
A melody plucked from the brightened moon.
With winks from aliens in a band,
We dance on stardust, hand in hand!

A serenade for comets that glide,
With funny hats on a joyride.
In orbits of giggles, we find our song,
As the universe joins in, all night long!

Cosmic Enigma

In a space where aliens dance,
They trip over lunar rocks by chance.
Worms in suits play cosmic chess,
With a referee who's kind of a mess.

Comets zoom with hair like mine,
Brushing past a moonlit sign.
"Don't feed the aliens!" it declares,
As I giggle at their silly stares.

Radiant Dreams

A twinkling light, a wobbly flight,
Where astronauts wear pajamas tight.
Floating pies in zero-gravity,
What a time to make some travesty!

Silly robots sing out of tune,
While dancing under a purple moon.
Their goofy moves make galaxies quake,
In this wacky universe, make no mistake!

In the Shadow of Giants

Under gigantic feet, we roam,
Wondering if they'll take us home.
With snacks in hand, we stand so proud,
In the shadow of a laughing cloud.

Riding meteors like a rollercoaster,
With a twist that feels like a toaster.
The giants giggle, they give a wave,
As we bounce, not knowing they misbehave.

Celestial Tapestry

In a quilt where planets intertwine,
Stitching dreams in the fabric of time.
Shooting fish swim, while leaping cows,
Stare in awe as gravity bows.

Jellybeans rain from a fiery sun,
With every scoop, we're having fun.
Orbiting oinks in a cosmic race,
Who knew the universe had such a face?

The Milky Veil

In cosmos where the giggles hide,
A comet tripped, it was quite a ride.
Dancing satellites in festive gowns,
Made all the moons laugh with their frowns.

A nebula sneezed, then glitter flew,
Making little asteroids shake and stew.
Galactic balloons began to pop,
And aliens rocked till they had to stop.

Tales of the Cosmic Tide

The sunbeams played hopscotch on the sphere,
While Saturn's rings twirled with a cheer.
The space fish were known to be quite sly,
They winked at passing comets flying by.

At cosmic fairs, they sold candy fluff,
And danced with quasars, who joined in the stuff.
With a wave of a hand and a pinch of sass,
They laughed at the weight of their swirling mass.

Nightfall Reverie

When dusk rolled in on a purple cloud,
The asteroids gathered, silly and loud.
They played silly games of tag and twirl,
While stardust sprinkled in a dizzy swirl.

A black hole tried to swallow the noise,
But only gobbled up a few space toys.
With giggles echoing through the vast,
The cosmic fun will always last.

Ethereal Doorways

Through portals shimmering with grit and glee,
We peeked at wacky worlds, one, two, three.
Ferrets in rocket ships zoomed past,
While jellybeans rained down, what a blast!

Pickles in spacesuits played a tune,
While muffins danced beside the moon.
In this quirky realm of giggles and fun,
Every oddball day had just begun.

Infinite Horizons

In the sky, a bright pinwheel,
Spinning tales of cosmic zeal.
Jupiter lost in a donut shop,
Eating rings, he just can't stop.

Aliens wearing funny hats,
Hosting parties and having chats.
Galaxies twirl in a salsa dance,
While comets glide, given the chance.

Light years drift like lazy clowns,
Bouncing off the moonlit towns.
Black holes sucking up the fun,
While rockets chase the setting sun.

The cosmos giggles, oh what a sight,
As asteroids throw a comet fight.
With space snacks floating all around,
In this universe, joy is found.

Starlit Pathways

Walking under a shiny quilt,
Made of dreams and cosmic guilt.
Space squirrels gather acorns bright,
Deciding who has the best flight.

Meteor showers rain down cheese,
While planets frolic in the breeze.
Saturn juggling its icy rings,
Laughing loud as the stardust sings.

Cosmic pizza slices fly,
Munching on them, time slips by.
Galactic giggles fill the air,
As rockets zoom without a care.

So join this dance of endless cheer,
A world where laughter's always near.
With every twinkle, joy expands,
In this play of cosmic hands.

The Universe Speaks

Listen close to the cosmic hum,
Whispers of wonders yet to come.
Nerdy aliens with glasses thick,
Debating which way to make a trick.

Supernovae pop like corn,
Lighting up the universe's lawn.
Planets wear their silly hats,
While Jupiter dances with the cats.

Aliens love a good joke told,
On a moon that's shining cold.
Asteroids make a ruckus loud,
Dressed as a wild and wacky crowd.

In whimsical orbits, comedy traps,
Galactic chuckles in time gaps.
And as they laugh, the cosmos sways,
In a comedic, starry ballet.

Orbital Dances

In a space disco, planets groove,
With comets cutting the best moves.
Neptune wears a golden shoe,
Twinkling brightly in the blue.

Satellites spin in a merry whir,
As space whales sing a tune to stir.
Light-speed limos zooming past,
Racing stars, they're built to last.

Asteroids trip in a clumsy waltz,
While gravity pulls and then exalts.
The moon is DJ, spinning tunes,
For a party that never balloons.

Black holes hide away in glee,
Sucking in jokes from A to Z.
So come join this cosmic craze,
And dance in the stellar haze!

Nurtured by the Night.

In the dark, where dreams are made,
Pajamas worn in a whimsical parade.
Pillow fights and silly grins,
Slumber parties, where fun begins.

Balloons float high, a silly sight,
Giggles echo, laughing in flight.
Secret snacks that we all share,
Midnight whispers, without a care.

Dancing shadows on the wall,
A blanket fort turns to a hall.
Imagination runs wild and free,
The night's our playground, just you and me.

As the morning sun peeks through,
We'll laugh about what we used to do.
A night so funny, we'll always recall,
Under moonlight, we had it all.

Celestial Whispers

Hopping 'round like hopping beans,
We giggle at what the cosmos means.
Twinkling lights on a giant screen,
Alien jokes that are simply obscene.

With a slurp and a giggle, we make a toast,
To moonlit soufflés, we love the most.
Chasing comets on a rocket scooter,
Your funny face? I call it a hooter!

Twirling under a neon sky,
With candy clouds drifting nearby.
Gravity? What a silly thing,
Let's dance until the night takes wing.

Galactic pranks from starry pranks,
We'll paint the sky with funny janks.
In this cosmic whirl, we're never alone,
With laughter as our guiding tone.

Cosmic Constellations

In the sky, shapes that twist and turn,
A cereal box whenever we yearn.
We draw with chalk on the pavement wide,
Our childish laughter, we can't hide.

A sock puppet show on a comet's tail,
With jellybeans spinning without fail.
Pretending to be astronauts with style,
In our cardboard ship, we travel a mile.

Silly stories of Martians and me,
Who dance around like they're on a spree.
Echoes of laughter, galloping through,
A parade of winks from me to you.

So let's look up and point with glee,
At the painted skies, you and me.
With our funny friends, we'll dance till noon,
Under the glow of a giggly moon.

Nighttime Serenade

When darkness falls, the fun ignites,
We sing to the moon on playful nights.
With flashlights waving like silly fans,
Making shadow puppets, doing our plans.

Whispers of giggles, a soft charade,
Under this blanket of peace, we've made.
We'll swap our stories, wild and wacky,
With every tale, the mood gets whacky.

Bouncing ideas like rubber balls,
As laughter echoes in distant halls.
The stories we tell are far from tame,
Each moment a picture, a frame in a game.

With snores and sighs, the night draws tight,
Yet in our dreams, we continue the fight.
For in this realm of sleep's embrace,
Funny visions of space fill our place.

Distant Flickers

In the night sky, odd shapes prance,
Little flickers, caught in a dance.
One's a burger, another's a cat,
I wonder if they know where they're at.

They giggle and twirl, shining quite bright,
Making silly faces, what a delight!
Chasing each other like kids on a swing,
Not caring at all about the chaos they bring.

A rocket ship zooms, with the crew all in jest,
Wearing pajamas, no time to rest.
They munch on some snacks and laugh 'til they snore,
Who knew being cosmic could be such a chore?

Then suddenly one trips, oh what a scene,
Falling through space like a wobbly bean.
The others just giggle, with no sense of care,
In the great sky circus, it's fun everywhere!

Celestial Journeys

Comets with tails made of cotton candy,
Sailing through voids, oh so dandy!
They stop for a snack on a nebula float,
Sharing their jellybeans, sugar-coated and wrote.

Planets in pairs play hide-and-seek,
One spins too fast, the other can't peek.
They tumble and roll, like kids on the grass,
Bumping and laughing, oh what a blast!

Galaxies dance in a twist and a whirl,
Meteors zooming, giving a twirl.
A space crab waves, with a wink and a grin,
Join in the fun, let the journey begin!

But watch out for asteroids, they throw quite the fit,
They'll dance on your head if you don't sidestep a bit.
So strut through the cosmos, with giggles and fun,
In this wacky adventure, you're never outdone!

Beyond the Firmament

Up in the blue, where the giggles go loud,
There's a party of fluff, a whimsical crowd.
Puppy-faced aliens, with candy cane hats,
Regaling each other with tales of their cats.

The sun becomes shy, paints a bright shade,
While a moonbeam juggles, making us laugh, unafraid.
They try to bake cookies with gravity's pull,
But end up with doughnuts - now that's quite the hull!

With laughter and light, they create a night show,
Performing suspended, all sparks and aglow.
A twinkling parade of quirks and delight,
Sprinkling some fun in the magical night.

But oh, here comes a galactic dance-off,
Each move sets off a cosmic cough.
As they tumble and fumble, the stars gently cheer,
In this boundless ballet, it's joy that's sincere!

Craters of Memory

On a distant path, with laughter to chase,
Are craters of fun, each shape brings a face.
One's a bowl of soup, the other a shoe,
Down the memory lane, I giggle anew.

Floating along, with marshmallows bright,
Reminiscing the shenanigans, sheer delight.
An alien chef spills spaghetti in space,
And chaos erupts, a real noodle race!

Each memento dangles like baubles on trees,
Wobbling and wobbling, swaying in the breeze.
Under a sky where jokes never die,
We savor those giggles, oh my, oh my!

So here's to the echoes, in laughter we find,
In craters of memory, we're all intertwined.
With dreams that keep spinning, like tops in a dance,
Let's leap through the cosmos, take another chance!

Night's Embrace

In the quiet of the night, we prance,
While aliens join us in a dance.
We sip our drinks from cosmic jars,
Laughing as we float 'neath glowing bars.

A raccoon wears a space suit tight,
Challenging us to a dance-off fight.
The moon snickers, with a wink so bright,
As we twirl around until first light.

Meteor showers rain down fries,
And we munch our snacks beneath pastel skies.
In this embrace of the cosmic fun,
We giggle until the night is done.

With laughter echoing through the void,
We celebrate the joy that's deployed.
Chasing our dreams through the galaxy,
In a night that feels like a rhapsody.

Echoes of the Void

Floating through space, we hear a cheer,
A funny voice saying, "Hey, I'm here!"
It's just a comet with shimmering flair,
Playing tricks with a laugh in the air.

Galactic jesters ride on stardust beams,
Slinging jokes like they're wild moonbeams.
An asteroid busted its best dad line,
'Why did the star break up? Too much shine!'

Zero-gravity games with waves of delight,
As we roll and tumble, it's pure dynamite.
We toss around jokes till the dawn appears,
And giggles echo through cosmic spheres.

In this black tapestry, humor's the thread,
As swirling planets tap dance overhead.
We gather stories from across the vast,
And cherish the joy that forever lasts.

Astral Wanderings

Wandering through the cosmic fringe,
A squirrel in space without a binge.
It juggles snacks as we fly by,
Underneath a jellybean sky.

A space llama wears a funky hat,
Stepping to rhythms that go chit-chat.
We join in and sway with grace,
Funky moves in this vast place.

With cheese from the moon, we feast and cheer,
Trying to share, but it disappears.
Galactic giggles fill the air,
As meteors crash without a care.

Through the cosmos, we spin and glide,
On a sparkly comet, we hilariously ride.
With twists and turns, our laughter rings,
For every day, the universe sings.

Celestial Celebrations

A party's brewing on a comet's tail,
With interstellar beings set to regale.
Pizza floats in a vacuum bliss,
A gravitational tug and a cheeky kiss.

Disco balls made from shimmery dust,
We boogie together, it's a cosmic must.
The planets join in with a funky beat,
As we groove on the dance floor, feeling sweet.

Cupcakes frosted with stardust sprinkles,
Bouncing around like cheerful twinkles.
Shooting confetti that never lands,
While alien friends lend their hands.

With laughter and cake, our hearts unite,
Celebrating life with pure delight.
In this celestial fest, joy holds sway,
As we twirl through the galaxy, come what may.

Shimmering Dreams

In the sky, the twinkle gleams,
Dancing lamps, oh how they beam!
Do they hold our wildest dreams?
Or just flashlights for moonbeams?

A cat in space, it seems so right,
Chasing orbs in the deep night.
What are those? A pizza slice?
Or cosmic cookies, oh so nice?

With ice cream cones for all the crew,
And chocolate rain, how sweet and blue!
Floating freely, what a view,
In this realm, we're all brand new!

So let's toast with fizzy wine,
And giggle at odd space design.
Intergalactic fun, divine,
On this dreamy path we shine!

Cosmic Ballet

A twirl and spin among the lights,
Waltzing comets, oh what sights!
Galaxies in tutus, spry,
Leaping through the cotton sky.

Meteor showers take a bow,
As asteroids jump, and how!
With tiny aliens in their suits,
Dancing clumsily in their boots.

A sunbeam front row takes its place,
Cheering on this wild embrace.
What a whimsical, grand affair,
In this dance, we lose all care!

Let's pirouette with no regret,
In a galaxy where dreams are met.
With every spin, we laugh and fret,
In this cosmic ballet, we're all set!

Luminous Legacies

From the glow of past mistakes,
To the shine of cosmic cakes.
An oven heated by the stars,
Baking treats in cookie jars.

What's that smell? A legacy,
Of burned toast in eternity!
With marshmallow rockets, take a ride,
Through zany worlds where giggles glide.

The echoes of a billion bloops,
As alien chefs stir space-soup groups.
Ladle out some laughter large,
In this bizarre veggie barge!

So raise a glass to glow and laugh,
To a universe that's quite daft!
With every light, a silly cheer,
In these legacies, we persevere!

The Unseen Voyage

On a journey not yet charted,
With a spaceship slightly parted.
What's that bump? Oh, just a snack!
An interstellar, crunchy pack!

Ghosts in orbit make a scene,
Telling jokes that aren't so clean.
With a wink and nod, they beam with glee,
Let's join them in this mystery!

Through wormholes filled with gummy bears,
And space whales singing truth or dares.
This ride won't end, no, not today,
As silly dreams lead us astray!

So buckle up, we're off to play,
In the cosmos where quirks hold sway.
An unseen voyage, what a treat,
With laughter ringing in every beat!

Galactic Journeys

In a rocket made of cheese,
We zoom past trees of candy leaves.
Martians wave with silly hats,
Sipping drinks from funky spats.

Asteroids dance, a cosmic jig,
We chuckle, oh, what a big gig!
Planets play hide and seek,
As comets race, they give a squeak.

Zooming by in a bubble car,
Spotting aliens at the interstellar bar.
Shooting stars pour cosmic ink,
A cosmic party, what do you think?

With wiggly tails and silly tunes,
The universe laughs and croons.
Oh, what a ride, what a spree!
In the space where we are free!

Celestial Dreams

In the night where giggles play,
Wobbly moons come out to sway.
Nebulas toss confetti bright,
In this world of pure delight.

Planets wear their party shoes,
While comets laugh, sharing news.
Supernovae burst in cheer,
While robots drink their root beer.

Asteroids roll like silly clowns,
Bumping into cosmic towns.
Galaxies twirl in a dance so grand,
As space dust settles on the land.

With sparkling trails and silly calls,
We'll bounce around in cosmic halls.
What a ride in this festive beam,
Living out our wildest dream!

Heavenly Ornaments

Hanging gems in the velvet sky,
Funky flying saucers zoom by.
Each twinkle a wink, each glow a smile,
Cosmic pranks that stretch a mile.

Jupiter juggles, oh what a sight,
Saturn's rings dance left and right.
Pluto plays hide and seek, so sly,
With ice cream cones that float nearby.

Galactic grins and goofy cheers,
Whirling and twirling through the years.
Comets wear hats that spin and twirl,
In a universe that loves to whirl.

With cosmic giggles and silly glee,
We'll celebrate eternally.
In this realm where laughter gleams,
Together we'll weave our silly dreams!

Lunar Echoes

On the moon, there's a silly show,
Bouncing bunnies in a row.
Galactic giggles echo wide,
As aliens join in the ride.

With wobbly walks and flips so high,
Floating cake comes sailing by.
Rockets blast with bursts of cheer,
While stardust sprinkles paint the sphere.

Martian munchies taste so fun,
As everyone joins in the run.
With glimmering lights and jolly tunes,
We'll dance beneath the glowing moons.

With laughter ringing through the night,
Every echo feels just right.
In our lunar land of joyful quests,
We'll party hard, just like the best!

Galactic Dreams

In pajamas with aliens, we fly,
While munching on space pies stacked high.
The astronauts giggle, and we all sway,
Orbiting planets in a dance hall way.

The rocket's on fire, but don't you fret,
We hold the controls like a cosmic pet.
With a wink and a chuckle, we'll blast through,
Floating to Pluto, just me and you.

Martian coffee served in a cup,
With jellybeans bouncing, oh what's up?
Zero-gravity plan for a game of tag,
Chasing comets in a shiny, sleek rag.

As we spin and trip in this endless whirl,
Just watch out for asteroids, they'll give you a twirl!
In this playful void, we laugh till we scream,
Living the life of our galactic dream.

Celestial Serenade

Singing with space squirrels, what a sight!
Dropping peanuts in the dark of night.
They twirl in the moonbeams, tails all a-fluff,
Telling tales of black holes, oh so gruff.

A comet with sunglasses zips past our way,
While the cosmos applaud, it's our cabaret.
We strum on the rings of a faraway giant,
Joking and laughing, the mood is defiant.

Astro-cats join in with a playful meow,
"Tune in!" they demand, "We need to wow!"
With a wink and a nod, we take center stage,
Sizzling star dances, a galactic page.

So grab your space hat, let's join in the fun,
With a sprinkle of sparkle from moonlight, we run.
In this serenade of celestial jest,
Together we'll sing, we forget all the rest.

Space Between Us

Zooming through tunnels of candy and light,
Dodging the constellations in flight.
A wink from a nebula, what a tease,
In this vast expanse, we do as we please.

Bouncing off comets, we giggle and roll,
A mishap with gravity took quite a toll.
Spinning like tops in the gravity-free zone,
Floating through dreams where we're never alone.

Jokes about aliens, oh what a ride,
In our little spaceship, goofy and wide.
With laughter that echoes through the dark of space,
Finding our rhythm in this cosmic race.

Between each laughter and furry delight,
We'll journey together, our bond feeling right.
In this expanse, weird and wonderful too,
The fun never ends, just me and you.

Constellation of Dares

In the dance of the cosmos, we take to the streets,
Challenging gravity with our wild, silly feats.
Daring each other to hop on a star,
Silly moonwalking, we're never too far.

Through craters and comets, we race at high speed,
Close encounters of laughter, oh yes indeed!
With a wink from a shooting star lighting the dark,
We're flipping our routines, what a whimsical spark.

"Catch me if you can!" I call from afar,
Now we're chasing space dogs—all that bizarre.
With interstellar giggles and silly cheer,
In this constellation of dares, have no fear!

As we tumble through night with our jokes and our pranks,
Navigating wormholes, giving ourselves thanks.
In the vastness of fun, we'll forever remain,
With laughter and love, we'll take on the insane.

Celestial Echoes

In the night, I see a light,
Flashing bright, what a sight!
It's a bug, a glowing bug,
Dancing 'round like it's snug.

Alien ships with pizza pies,
Zooming past, oh what a rise!
They serve sauce from a can,
A funny galactic plan!

Rockets made of candy bars,
Taking off to dance with stars.
But wait, they forgot their hats,
Now they float with silly spats.

So laugh with me, let's take flight,
On this trip, everything's light!
The universe is quite absurd,
With laughter echoing unheard.

Galactic Avenues

Down the streets of cosmic dust,
I saw a comet with a crust.
It asked me for a friendly snack,
I offered chips, but got a whack.

Martians on scooters zoom by fast,
Trying to catch a comet's blast.
They giggle, wobble, spill their tea,
But they won't share, oh woe is me!

Spaceships shaped like giant ducks,
Quacking tunes, what funny luck!
With laser beams that shoot confetti,
They bring joy that's always ready.

Avenue of shimmery dreams,
Where nothing's ever as it seems.
So join this wacky cosmic fun,
Under the glow of a silly sun.

The Twilight Realm

In the twilight, shadows peek,
While planets wink and softly speak.
I think I saw a moonwalk here,
   An alien dressed up as a deer.

Worms with shades, they twist and twirl,
They really know how to give a whirl!
One wore socks that didn't match,
   It's the latest cosmic catch.

Jellybeans rain in the night,
A sugar storm is such a sight!
Galactic dances, all askew,
A cosmic party just for you.

So twirl around in this strange land,
With gummy walls and lemon sand.
Here, every laugh is quite absurd,
   In this realm, joy is the word.

Nebula Reflections

In a cloud of cotton candy,
I found a creature, oh so handy!
It borrowed my hat for the show,
Leaving me with quite a woe.

Planets chuckled at my loss,
As I searched like a silly boss.
I tripped on an asteroid's cheese,
And rolled down with a loud wheeze!

Bubbles floated, soft and bold,
One popped! It sprayed out gold.
My new friend laughed, what a sight,
Together we sparkled in the night.

So join this cosmic chase,
Where giggles light up all the space.
Reflections of laughter, pure delight,
In the nebula of the night.

Celestial Mosaic

In the sky, a twinkling sight,
A dance of sparks in the night.
Wandering cows say 'moo', then pause,
They think they see the Milky Cause.

A rabbit hops from a giant pod,
With a carrot hat he gives a nod.
They shoot for cheese, oh, what a thrill,
When they land, it's a backward drill!

Galactic pies floating on plates,
Aliens serve them on date-like dates.
With whipped cream comets on top, do share,
Eat it fast, don't float in air!

Jellybeams and gummy rays,
Whirling around in cosmic plays.
A ticklish worm rides a light beam,
Who knew the void holds such a dream?

The Interstellar Tide

Five-eyed fish swim in soda streams,
Catching bubbles, plotting schemes.
With a popcorn moon, they take a dive,
Who knew space could be so alive?

Custard planets roll like balls,
Planets dressed for disco calls.
Galactic tunes make them groove,
Watch out, black holes start to move!

Marshmallow meteors zoom with glee,
Landing on cupcakes—yummy spree!
Shooting jelly beans across the night,
Candy comets in a comical flight.

Bubbling broth of cosmic soup,
Where starry giggles create a loop.
Dancing ducks in rocket shoes,
In this space, there's nothing to lose!

Night's Mystique

Bunnies bounce on fluffy clouds,
Wearing shades and laughing loud.
Cats in spacesuits chase a kite,
While gnomes sell snacks that are out of sight!

Squirrels driving tiny cars,
Making wishes on cosmic jars.
With chunky chocolate sprinkles near,
This galactic party brings good cheer!

Chubby aliens on pogo sticks,
Juggling giggles and banana tricks.
They sing of cheese and dance in glee,
A night like this is a fine decree!

With a wink and a tickling breeze,
The cosmos plays on, such a tease.
Where laughter echoes through the void,
And goofy wonders can't be avoided!

Beyond the Celestial Sphere

What lies beyond, a fuzzy haze,
With rubber ducks in a cosmic maze.
A taco spaceship zooms and swirls,
With chocolate aliens and peppermint curls.

Invisible friends toss glittering beams,
While marshmallow meteors bounce in dreams.
Fairies race with cosmic gear,
Waving to toasters that hover near.

Balloons of laughter fill the void,
In this realm, there's nothing to avoid.
Sundae stars with sprinkles bright,
Gather round for a silly night.

So hold your spoons, take a leap,
For cosmic delights, we'll always keep.
In this infinite playground, let's embark,
Where joy and weirdness make their mark!

Beyond the Event Horizon

In the cosmos, a galactic show,
Where lost socks and dust bunnies flow.
Planets rolling like dice in the air,
While aliens snicker, "Is this a fair?"

Black holes munch on space-time treats,
Grinning comets on sugar rush feats.
Gravity pulls on my silly hat,
As I float by with a zany spat!

Wormholes twist like pretzels spun,
Chasing stars like they're just for fun.
I tripped on a quasar's beam so bright,
"Oops!" I said, "Is this a flight?"

In zero-G, my hair's a fluff,
Floating like jelly, but never enough.
Just another day in this cosmic jest,
Where laughter echoes and puns manifest!

Starlit Odysseys

On a journey through the glittering sea,
I lost my map, now I'm just free.
Navigating by snacks I've amassed,
Munching on stardust, it's quite a blast!

Planets wave, trying hard to dance,
While I'm busy chuckling at my own prance.
Spaceships zoom by, honking the horn,
"Cap'n, where are we?" I yawn and scorn!

I bumped into a giant moon cheese,
"Excuse me, hope you find this a breeze."
But the moon just chuckled, "You're quite the fool,
I guess it's not lunch; it's cosmic school!"

Nebulas swirl, painting the sky,
While asteroids wink as they zip by.
With giggles echoing through the night,
It's a silly adventure, pure delight!

The Call of the Universe

Out there in the void, a loud 'hello!'
I answered back with a goofy throw.
The cosmos replied with a rumble of cheers,
"Grab your space outfit, dance away fears!"

Shooting stars play tag over sunlit roofs,
While little green beings show off their moves.
"Step right up!" they beckon with glee,
"Join us for a round of cosmic tee-hee!"

Cosmic jazz fills the air so wild,
As I spin around like a dizzy child.
Comedy routines from comets up high,
Leave my sides aching from laughing, oh my!

A wand'rer appears, juggling moons with flair,
"Care for a laugh? It's a stellar affair!"
It's a universe where giggles take flight,
As laughter echoes into the night.

Dreaming Under Canopies

Beneath swirling whirlpools of twinkling sheen,
I dream of wonders, where I've never been.
Clouds of cotton candy float soft and light,
While I sip on starlight, my heart feels bright!

Giggles from afar seem to dance and play,
As lunar fireflies set the night ablaze.
"Come join us!" the whispers gently implore,
"Dreams blend in colors, and never bore!"

Cosmic slides sweep through the skies of hue,
Where fun is the language, and joy's never due.
Wishing on wishes, while laughter takes flight,
Everything's wacky 'neath the canopy light.

Planets join hands in a playful parade,
All wear silly hats and are not afraid.
Under this canopy, smiles are the prize,
In a whimsical world where happiness flies!

Twilight Dances

In twilight's glow, we trip and fall,
Gravity's stubborn, it calls us all.
With silly hats and mismatched socks,
We dance like fish, and race like clocks.

The moon chuckles, it can't believe,
Our wobbly moves that make it grieve.
We spin like tops, quite out of sync,
And laugh until we start to wink.

Echoes Across the Void

In emptiness, our laughter rings,
Like rubber ducks on rubber strings.
Each echo bounces, wild and free,
It's music made by you and me.

We toss our voices, let them soar,
Like silly balloons from a store.
The silence giggles as we shout,
Unusual fun, without a doubt.

Celestial Reverberations

Dancing comets and flying pies,
The sky erupts in funny cries.
With cosmic muffins, we celebrate,
And spin around on our own plate.

We play poker with little green guys,
As they pull pranks and tell wild lies.
The universe laughs, it's quite a sight,
When aliens dance through the starry night.

The Infinite Waltz

In a ballroom made of glitter and cheers,
We waltz through time, ignoring fears.
With goofy grins and polka socks,
Our two left feet dance with the clocks.

We twirl through timeless, cheeky schemes,
And giggle softly, lost in dreams.
The universe's floor is our own,
In this strange place where laughter's grown.

Lightyears from Home

In a rocket that smells like cheese,
Floating past Uranus with ease.
My pet goldfish is the pilot,
Every twist makes me feel like riot.

I thought I'd see aliens, fun and bright,
Instead, it's just space glitter in sight.
With comet trails making me sneeze,
I wonder if they have pizza, if you please.

The universe laughs with a twinkle and wink,
As I sip on my freeze-dried drink.
A passing asteroid gives a cheeky smile,
While I float in my spaceship, quite a while.

So here I drift, far from the shore,
With a rubber chicken and space to explore.
Next stop, the moon, for a dance and a joke,
In this backyard of space, I'm an intergalactic bloke!

Cosmic Sonnet

Oh rocket man with your goggles so fine,
Your head's in the clouds, the universe divine.
Juggling meteors while playing the flute,
Impressing Martians with a galactic loot.

Your spaceship's a mess, just a box full of fluff,
Space travel is wild, but it's also real tough.
With every new orbit, your socks start to smell,
But you swear that they're charming, just quirky and swell.

Aliens swing by for a cup and a chat,
While your cat does the tango, how 'bout that?
You dig into stardust, take playful bites,
And laugh at the moon, oh what funny sights!

So charge up your rocket, grab a pie on the fly,
Let's trade silly jokes as we zoom through the sky.
This cosmic adventure is full of delight,
Remember, it's fun, keep your humor in sight!

The Celestial Prelude

With a twirl and a whirl, the planets descend,
In a cosmic ballet, will you be my friend?
A comet hiccups as it zips on by,
While I wear my telescope like a goofy tie.

Floating through nebulae, colors collide,
Wormholes are shortcuts for a fun cosmic ride.
My shoes are all sticky from space-gummy bears,
And the aliens keep me with their funny stares.

A black hole appears, but I'm not feeling gloom,
It's just a troupe of space clowns ready to zoom!
They juggle the galaxies with spaghetti strings,
And offer me mooncakes with bright little wings.

So grab your seatbelt, and let's take a chance,
To shimmy through space in a twinkly dance.
The universe chuckles, a party so grand,
With laughter and joy, hand in hand!

Luminous Pathways

In a rocket fueled by dreams and a laugh,
I zoom past bright wonders, on a whimsical path.
Each planet's a party, a cake and a game,
Where everyone's welcome, no one's the same.

The moons play tag, while the asteroids race,
With space squirrels handing out snacks full of grace.
I wore a green tutu, much to their surprise,
And danced with the comets beneath starlit skies.

Oh, how fun it is to float without care,
While aliens giggle, with colorful hair.
We share silly stories, of trips gone awry,
And bounce through the cosmos, just you and I.

So let's chart a course on this jolly delight,
Exploring the night with our hearts shining bright.
In this cosmic carnival, we'll laugh and we'll play,
Creating a journey that's silly each day!

Shadows of the Cosmos

In the night sky, a cat takes flight,
Chasing cheese with all its might.
Planets giggle, they swirl and twirl,
While comets dress in sparkly whirl.

Jupiter paints with broccoli green,
Mercury's stuck in a soap bubble scene.
A rocket ship plays hopscotch with fate,
But the aliens just can't wait!

Galaxies burp like they're at a feast,
Shooting stars spill juice, not the least.
They juggle moons like circus clowns,
In leather jackets and silly frowns.

Black holes snicker, they're in on the joke,
Sucking in laughter with each poke.
While light beams giggle, taking a bow,
In this cosmic circus, oh wow, wow, wow!

Far Beyond the Horizon

Beyond the line where the sea meets the sky,
Lies a pickle spaceship that flies oh so high.
Seagulls wear hats, and fish read the news,
While crabs under umbrellas sip lemony brews.

The sun wears shades, it's looking quite cool,
Doing the limbo around a bright pool.
Mermaids debate about who has the best,
Funny seaweed, they put to the test.

Clouds canoodle like marshmallows sweet,
As dolphins tap dance with two left feet.
A whale sings opera, quite off-key,
But everyone laughs, so free and so breezy.

With horizons laughing and splashing around,
Each wave is a pun, each crest is a sound.
So sail away, let the humor excite,
In the big silly ocean, where day meets the night!

A Dance of Light

Flickering fireflies in tutus so bright,
Spin under the moon, what a curious sight.
Flashlight fairies hold a grand ball,
With glow-worms invited, they all have a ball.

Twinkling lights strut in a heavenly line,
Doing the cha-cha, sipping on wine.
Nebulas launch into a funky schmooze,
While asteroids rock their dad-bod blues.

Cosmic conga with a starry-eyed grin,
Who knew that space was this much fun to spin?
With each little twirl, a collision is near,
But no one gets hurt; they just bring a cheer!

Dancing in sync, they wobble and sway,
A kaleidoscope whirl, come join in the play.
In this cosmic jamboree, laughter ignites,
It's a frolicsome waltz, where joy takes flight!

Between the Worlds

In a realm where the odd meets the bizarre,
A toaster is zapping, a dancing guitar.
The sun wears goggles, the moon in a cape,
And tea parties with robots, oh what a shape!

Puppies in space with bubblegum treats,
Chasing space cheese that nobody eats.
There's laughter in echoes, a whimsical game,
As dragons in tutus play tag with no shame.

The doors of dimensions are swinging with flair,
Inviting all critters from here and from there.
One-eyed aliens roller-skate by,
While squirrels in helmets take off to the sky.

So leap through the portals, come explore with me,
In this wacky wonderland of glee!
Where each twist and turn brings giggles anew,
Between the worlds, it's a hullabaloo!

Planets in Pursuit

A comet chased a cow with glee,
While asteroids danced, wild and free.
Celestial critters played a game,
Their antics always brought them fame.

Venus tripped on Saturn's rings,
Jupiter laughed at all her flings.
Uranus giggled, what a sight,
As they whirled in cosmic light.

Cosmic cows in zero-gravity,
The galaxy's own comedy.
With space pies flying through the air,
And aliens in tutus, oh so rare!

At dusk, they had a party grand,
With snacks from some far-off, funny land.
Their laughter echoed through the void,
In this funny realm, none were paranoid.

Ethereal Alignments

A giant whale swam in the sky,
With sparkly wings that made you sigh.
While gnomes danced on comet tails,
And floated high in funny sails.

A unicorn flew by wearing shades,
While singing tunes that never fade.
Gargoyles played hopscotch on asteroids,
Creating games with cosmic joys.

Aliens in tuxedos twirled,
With disco balls that spun and swirled.
They had a ball, oh what a night,
As they grooved to spacey light.

When the planets aligned just right,
With giggles echoing through the night.
We'll party 'til the sun comes home,
In this cosmic dance, we freely roam.

Neon Nightscapes

Underneath a glow so bright,
Where jellybeans take flight at night.
Marshmallow clouds float by in rows,
As laughter tickles all the toes.

With rainbow wishes and moonlit beams,
Chasing wacky, whimsical dreams.
Bright balloons and shining snacks,
Fluffy creatures in playful packs.

The candy comet zooms around,
In this fun, sweet playground.
While vibrant lights light up the sky,
With giggles that make the planets sigh.

Astro-bunnies hop with flair,
In this nightscape, full of air.
Join the dance, don't be shy,
Under the neon, oh me, oh my!

Astral Pathways

On rainbow paths where laughter flows,
A parade of planets, grandiose shows.
Puppies dressed as Martians prance,
While stars and comets join the dance.

Galactic trains with candy cars,
Pulling dreams from distant stars.
Light years melt in a sweet embrace,
As silly faces fill the space.

Wormholes spun like carnival rides,
In this cosmic fun where joy abides.
With candy corn in every breeze,
And jellyfish doing the limbo with ease.

As we glide on pathways bright,
Our chuckles echo through the night.
So grab a friend and take a trip,
In this astral world, we'll never slip.

Whispers of Infinity

In the night, a twinkling light,
A comet passes, what a sight!
A rocket left, a cat took charge,
Now it seems we've lost the barge.

Jupiter's got a stormy cloak,
While Saturn laughs and cracks a joke.
Aliens dance with cosmic glee,
Bet they laugh, just wait and see!

Galaxies swirl, a party brew,
With moon pies tossed and space tacos too.
Yet here we sit, so blissfully mad,
Imagining worlds that make us glad.

Comets kiss the silvery dew,
As astronauts lose their lunch, it's true!
And in the end, we find our threads,
Woven in dreams, as fun abeds.

Cosmic Landmarks

A palace built on an asteroid,
With rubber duckies, how we enjoyed!
Space penguins slide down black hole whirl,
Laughing as they twirl and twirl.

Rings of ice and clouds of gas,
An alien band plays off the sass.
Mars drinks a soda, giggling loud,
Promising to land, oh-so-proud!

Constellations wave their arms,
Every wink is filled with charms.
A selfie taken, the stars align,
"Look at us!" they gleefully whine.

Stardust trails like sprinkles fall,
As spacemen answer nature's call.
With cosmic pizzas spinning high,
You'd think we'd reach for the sky!

Timeless Celestial Ballads

A solar flare dances with flair,
While Pluto hums without a care.
The asteroids play hide and seek,
Chasing tails with comets so sleek!

Quasars shout with a booming voice,
"Join our party!" We rejoice.
Galactic clowns juggle bright moons,
While Earthlings sing silly tunes.

With craters that look like silly hats,
And bouncing rocks like playful chats,
The universe keeps its groove alive,
In a comedy beyond, a jive!

As space whales swim through the dark,
They hum a tune, a song, a lark.
And if you listen, you may find,
The cosmic giggles, hilariously kind.

Hues of the Infinite

Lavender lights in a nebula's haze,
Galactic gnomes in a cosmic maze.
Banana trees on a distant sun,
And space cats know how to have fun!

Blue moons with polka dots, so bold,
A wacky tale of stardust told.
Alien fish dance in zero G,
Twisting and turning, oh what a spree!

Nebula parties with cupcakes bright,
An orbiting chef, just out of sight.
"More sprinkles!" yells a Martian gal,
As we all laugh at the cosmic pal.

With color swirls that light the night,
And cosmic creatures that bring delight.
Every glance at the sky feels right,
In the joy of laughter, we take flight!

Celestial Whispers

In the sky, a twinkling jest,
A cosmic giggle, quite the quest.
Planets roll their sleepy eyes,
As comets whirl with belly cries.

The moon plays tricks, a playful light,
Winks at shadows, oh what a sight!
Galaxies swirl in a silly race,
While aliens wear a funny face.

Cosmic Boundaries

Across the void, a joke takes flight,
A spaceship stumbles, what a fright!
Asteroids chuckle, drifting around,
While meteors dance, not making a sound.

Light years stretch like a rubber band,
A cosmos where silliness is grand.
Infinity giggles, can you hear?
In the distance, the laughter's near.

Red Planet Reverie

On a dusty orb, a game unfolds,
Martians tease with stories bold.
They sip on drinks of cosmic brew,
And shake their heads at Earthlings too.

Rovers trip on hidden rocks,
Tumbling over, pulling socks.
The landscape smiles, no reason to frown,
As space dust dances, up and down.

Night Sky Chronicles

With a wink from the velvet deep,
Celestial critters plot and creep.
A shooting star, a clumsy guide,
Trips over space, now where to hide?

Galactic tales of laughter's gain,
Echo softly, like a raindrop's lane.
In this tapestry of cosmic fun,
Every twinkle knows when day is done.

Cracks in the Cosmos

In the sky, a pizza slice,
Where did the toppings go?
Did aliens munch them up?
Or did they just say 'no'?

With a sprinkle of stardust,
And a comet for a pie,
We throw a cosmic party,
Watch the meteors fly by.

Planets dance in silly shoes,
While black holes spin and twirl,
Making friends with every quasar,
In a dizzy, funny whirl.

So when you gaze at night, my friend,
And wonder what's up there,
Just know it's not all serious,
Some laughter's in the air.

Light between the Galaxies

In the dark there's a glow,
Like fireflies on parade,
Connecting dotted lines of dreams,
A celestial charade.

Neon comets zooming past,
With giggles in their wake,
And every light an inside joke,
For the universe's sake.

Through the void, a wink occurs,
As time bends like a straw,
The space-time continuum laughs,
At its own funny law.

So grab your flashlight, let's explore,
The humor that's in flight,
Between the galaxies and dreams,
We'll shine till morning light.

Infinite Landscapes

Clouds of cotton candy float,
On a taffy sunset grand,
Where lollipop trees sway gently,
In a candy-coated land.

The rivers run with chocolate milk,
And gumdrops line the street,
With cosmic jellybeans to munch,
Oh, what a tasty treat!

Marshmallow mountains rise and fall,
While jellyfish have a dance,
In this bizarre, infinite place,
Everything's a funny chance.

So take a trip where logic bends,
And taste the cosmic cheer,
With every bite, a giggle bursts,
In landscapes far and near.

The Great Expanse

Beyond the rockets' noisy roar,
And satellites that tease,
There's a place where ducks wear hats,
And float on cosmic breeze.

Spaceships shaped like rubber ducks,
With engines made of ice,
Zoom past giants swinging clubs,
A game that's not so nice.

The vacuum hums a funny tune,
As planets glide on skates,
While meteors tumble, laugh and spin,
In this vast, silly state.

So if you hear a cosmic joke,
Or see a shooting star,
Just know the universe is bright,
And laughter's never far.

Ethereal Landscapes

In a land where oddities roam,
Space cows chew gum at home.
Silly critters jump and dance,
While aliens join in their prance.

Giant pizzas float above,
Saucy, cheesy, full of love.
They sing a tune, oh what a sight,
While moonbeams giggle through the night.

Convert the beach into a wave,
Surfing comets, daring and brave.
A marshmallow sun on the rise,
Puffing dreams in the starry skies.

With a wink, the stardust plays,
In goofy suits and goofy ways.
Hitchhiking through the great unknown,
Creating joy wherever it's shown.

The Light Between Worlds

Cocktail planets spin and twirl,
Dressed in sparkles, they unfurl.
Rainbows splash like frothy waves,
As you join the cosmic knaves.

A giraffe in shades joins the fun,
Twirling beneath a blushing bun.
Giggles echo from afar,
Where no one looks like they are.

Mirrors break with gleeful shouts,
Echoing in spirals and bouts.
The universe wraps you tight,
In a giggly, bouncy flight.

Unicorns hosting tea parties,
With donuts shaped like ancient artifacts.
Count the jellybeans that tumble,
In this realm where no one fumbles.

Beyond the Blue Veil

Through a curtain of giggles and laughs,
A walrus plays with goofy gaffs.
Balloons float in a whimsical breeze,
As jellyfish join on their knees.

Rain falls up, it's quite absurd,
The sun scribbles, it feels unheard.
Birds wear hats that flutter by,
As squirrels in tuxedos wave goodbye.

Waffle cones sprout legs to dance,
While nutty clowns join the prance.
Complaints of gravity get no ear,
In this realm of funk and cheer.

Teleporting like a wobbly ball,
Down rabbit holes they dance and crawl.
Cracks in time, a silly twist,
As normal fades into the mist.

Planetary Odyssey

Planet hop on a giant shoe,
Wobbling under skies so blue.
Cosmic giggles fill the air,
As otters pull their best neck hair.

Rocket pops take off with flair,
While penguins swim without a care.
Toasty marshmallows in the way,
Waving hello, they come to play.

Silly sounds of spacey cheers,
As quirky jokes ignite the gears.
Beware the moons that love to tease,
With puns that echo through the trees.

So hop aboard, let's take a ride,
Across the galaxy, wild and wide.
With laughter as our guiding star,
Who knows just how grand we are!

Portals to the Infinite

Rockets in pajamas zoom through the sky,
Chasing donuts as they float by.
Alien squirrels with nuts in their paws,
Laugh as they break all of our laws.

Wormholes are just slides for galactic play,
Chasing bright comets, what a wild day!
With every great leap we twist and we twirl,
Until we collide with a space-time girl.

Insect-sized astronauts riding on beams,
Hold on tight, it's all just dreams!
As meteors sing and planets dance,
We find ourselves lost in a cosmic romance.

So let's toast to nights where silliness reigns,
With Milky Way snacks and asteroid gains.
In this universe, fun's always the goal,
When we're zipping through space on a chocolate roll.

Celestial Melodies

Jupiter jives to a funky beat,
While Saturn grooves on its ringed feet.
Pluto plays hide-and-seek with the sun,
Laughing together, oh what fun!

Shooting stars trade their best jokes,
While cosmic winds dance with carefree folks.
Neptune's voice is a lovely tune,
As it serenades the glowing moon.

Galactic giggles echo in space,
As meteors throw a silly race.
With stardust confetti scattered around,
We're lost in this party, don't make a sound!

Each twinkle and glimmer, a chuckle shared,
In the velvet sky, life is rarely dared.
With cosmic laughter lighting the way,
Join the fun, let's play all day!

Lost in the Nebula

In a cosmic cloud, we tumble and spin,
With marshmallow comets, let the games begin!
Giggling gas giants in fluffy attire,
Disrupting the order with cosmic satire.

Spaceships made of candy zip through the mist,
Searching for planets that can't be missed.
Bubblegum asteroids with silly names,
Kicking up dust in hilarious games.

Nebula secrets wrapped in bright hues,
While twinkling stars read the funniest news.
We're lost in the chaos, but loving the ride,
In this whimsical dance, we'll always slide.

So pack up your smiles and laughter, my friend,
Join our adventure—there's no need to pretend.
Through giggles and glares, our journey's a blast,
In this cosmic comedy, we're having a blast!

Whispering Echoes

Voices of moons call out with delight,
Making echoes in the blanket of night.
Silly shadows play tricks on your eyes,
   As we ponder the fate of a comet pie.

Galaxies chirp in a language of fun,
While stardust settles, we all start to run.
Chasing the laughter that lingers in air,
With planetary pinatas, no worries, no care.

Riding on rays of sunlight so free,
Tickling the cosmos, just you and me.
As planets align for a cosmic shindig,
We make merry mischief, a frolic, a big!

With whimsical whispers that flutter about,
Our fantastical friends never seem to doubt.
In the symphony of space, we truly rejoice,
With echoes of laughter, we add to the noise.